W9-BYQ-011

NASCAR RACING

Dale Earnhardt

by A. R. Schaefer

Consultant:
Suzanne Wise, Librarian
Stock Car Racing Collection, Belk Library
Appalachian State University
Boone, North Carolina

Capstone press®

Mankato, Minnesota

Dale's expert driving skills made him a NASCAR legend.

He bumped Dale again on the next lap, but Dale held onto the lead. On the next lap, Elliott hit Dale again on purpose. This time he hit him hard enough to knock him off the racetrack.

Dale's car headed into the grass below the track. He could have put on the brakes and slowly climbed back onto the track. Instead, Dale stepped on the accelerator. He plowed through 150 feet (46 meters) of grass at more than 150 miles (241 kilometers) per hour. When he got back on the track, he still had the lead.

The move shocked fans and other drivers. Dale didn't give up his position and went on to win the race. People call the move "The Pass in the Grass." Many fans consider it the greatest move in NASCAR history.

Dale Earnhardt

Dale Earnhardt was one of the legends of NASCAR. Many people consider him the greatest stock car driver ever. He won seven NASCAR Cup championships and 76 Cup races.

Dale felt at home behind the wheel of a stock car.

People knew Dale for his bold driving style. While other drivers stayed back and waited for something to happen, Dale charged ahead. He took risks other drivers wouldn't take. Fans either loved him or hated him because of his aggressive style on the track.

Dale belonged to one of the best-known racing families. His father was a famous NASCAR driver, and his sons and daughter have also raced.

"The greatest move in the history of auto racing. To be driving a car that fast on the grass? To keep control? That was unbelievable."
—Humpy Wheeler, Charlotte Motor Speedway president, *At the Altar of Speed*

CHAPTER 2

Early Start

Many people say that Dale Earnhardt was born to race stock cars. He grew up in the area of the country where stock car racing began. He also was born into a family that raced stock cars for a living.

Racing Father

Dale was born April 29, 1951, in Kannapolis, North Carolina. He lived near Kannapolis his entire life. His father, Ralph, was one of the first NASCAR drivers. Ralph was also a successful driver.

For Dale, racing stock cars was something he was born to do.

Learn about:

→ Ralph Earnhardt
→ Learning the sport
→ Dale's first race car

Dale learned about racing by watching his father. At age 10, Dale started going with Ralph to races. He watched the races from the top of a truck. He paid attention to the moves the drivers used.

Learning the Ropes

As a teenager, Dale worked on his father's car. First, he helped repair it in the garage at home. Later, he became a part of Ralph's pit crew. He enjoyed being part of a racing team. He worked for his father for several years. At age 19, Dale drove his brother-in-law's spare race car. He competed in his first race in 1970, on a dirt track.

"I didn't like school, I wanted to be home cleaning up the shop."
—Dale Earnhardt, June 2001,
Circle Track magazine

Career Statistics

Dale Earnhardt

Year	Starts	Wins	Top 5s	Top 10s	Winnings
1975	1	0	0	0	$2,425
1976	2	0	0	0	$3,085
1977	1	0	0	0	$1,375
1978	5	0	1	2	$20,745
1979	27	1	11	17	$274,810
1980	31	5	19	24	$671,990
1981	31	0	9	17	$353,971
1982	30	1	7	12	$400,880
1983	30	2	9	14	$465,203
1984	30	2	12	22	$634,670
1985	28	4	10	16	$546,595
1986	29	5	16	23	$1,768,880
1987	29	11	21	24	$2,069,243
1988	29	3	13	19	$1,214,089
1989	29	5	14	19	$1,432,230
1990	29	9	18	23	$3,308,056
1991	29	4	14	21	$2,416,685
1992	29	1	6	15	$915,463
1993	30	6	17	21	$3,353,789
1994	31	4	20	25	$3,300,733
1995	31	5	19	23	$3,154,241
1996	31	2	13	17	$2,285,926
1997	32	0	7	16	$2,151,909
1998	33	1	5	13	$2,990,749
1999	34	3	7	21	$3,048,236
2000	34	2	13	24	$4,918,886
2001	1	0	0	0	$296,833
Career	676	76	281	428	$42,001,697

The car was a lot different from the number 3 car that he would be known for later. The old Ford sedan went into the shop for a coat of green paint. But the workers mixed the paint wrong. The first car Dale ever drove in a professional race was pink. It was an unusual start for a man who would later drive a black car and be called the Intimidator.

"It seems like I was put here to drive a race car. I was bred and raised to do that."
—Dale Earnhardt, June 2001, *Circle Track* magazine

Dale's black Monte Carlo became famous. It was a far cry from the first car he ever drove.

CHAPTER 3

Breaking Out

During his first few years of racing, Dale mostly stayed close to home and raced on dirt tracks. Sometimes he traveled to South Carolina, Virginia, or Tennessee for a race. Many races were in North Carolina. His first win came at Concord Speedway, just a few miles from Kannapolis.

Dale didn't make a lot of money racing, so he had other jobs. For a while he worked at a wheel alignment shop. He was a welder. Dale did anything to make enough money to keep his car running. Sometimes he took out loans to buy parts for his car.

Dale's early races were in the Sportsman division.

Learn about:

→ Sportsman division
→ Rookie of the year
→ NASCAR championship

17

Big Step

In 1974, Dale decided to try racing on pavement. He prepared a car for a Sportsman race. Today, the Sportsman division is called the Busch Series. Some weeks, Dale raced in several Busch races.

In 1975, a NASCAR Cup team had an extra car for the World 500 in Charlotte, North Carolina. The Cup used to be called the Winston Cup. Someone suggested that Dale drive it. Even though he was in an older car, Dale finished 22nd in his first race and made more than $1,925. He raced in a few more Cup races in the next three years. But he raced in older cars and never could break out of the pack.

Dale won his first NASCAR points championship in 1980.

Finally, in the second to the last race of the 1978 season, Dale got his big break. A rich owner from California had a new car that he wanted Dale to drive at Atlanta. Dale finished fourth. After the season, the owner asked Dale to drive it full-time in 1979.

First Win

Once Dale got into a good car, it didn't take him long to win. In only his 16th Cup start, Dale won the seventh race of the 1979 season at Bristol. That year, he finished seventh in the points standings and won more than $264,000. Dale was named Rookie of the Year. He was on his way to being a star.

The next year, Dale had a breakout year. He won back-to-back races in Atlanta and Bristol early in the season. He won three more races later that season. He stayed in first place in the standings almost the whole season. Dale won his first NASCAR Cup Series points championship in only his second full-time year. He took home more than $500,000.

CHAPTER 4

An Amazing Career

After his first championship, Dale was seen as a driver to beat. Things wouldn't continue to go so well though. The owner from California decided to get out of NASCAR. Without the owner, everything changed for Dale. It would be years before he would win another championship.

Changing Teams

In 1982 and 1983, Dale drove for a different owner. He felt uncomfortable driving the owner's cars. They often broke. He couldn't drive the way he wanted if he felt the car wouldn't hold up. He only won three races in those two years.

Dale won more races after he began racing for the Childress team.

Learn about:

→ The Ford years
→ A new team
→ Daytona

Dale celebrates a win with team owner Richard Childress.

At the end of the 1983 season, Dale signed a contract with team owner Richard Childress. It may have been the best decision he ever made.

The Childress team's goal was to build tough race cars. These cars worked well with Dale's aggressive driving style. Childress cars took hits that sent other cars to the garage. The team dominated the NASCAR Cup Series in 1986 and 1987. In 1986, Dale won five races and the championship. In 1987, he won 11 races. He won the championship again. Dale would win the championship four more times in 1990, 1991, 1993, and 1994.

Daytona

Even though he had won seven NASCAR Cup Series championships by 1994, Dale had never won the biggest race of the season. He won at Daytona many times, but never won the Daytona 500. Finally, in 1998, Dale won the race. People were very happy for him. Pit crews from other teams even lined up on pit road to congratulate him.

Dale Earnhardt will forever be linked to Daytona International Speedway. He won 29 races there during his career. But something happened to him there that changed NASCAR forever. On the last lap of the 2001 Daytona 500, Dale got tangled with some other cars. He crashed into the wall. Dale was killed in the crash.

Dale was involved in a fatal crash during the 2001 Daytona 500.

During his career, Dale won seven NASCAR Cup Series championships. He is tied for the all-time record with Richard Petty. Dale won 76 Cup races. His black number 3 Monte Carlo was one of the most familiar sights in racing. He drove with an aggressive style that his fans will never forget.

The Earnhardts

The Earnhardt family is one of the most famous racing families in NASCAR. Ralph Earnhardt and Dale Earnhardt were named two of NASCAR's 50 greatest drivers. Dale's children are also involved in racing. His oldest son, Kerry, has raced in Cup and Busch Series races. Dale's daughter, Kelly, raced for a while. His younger son, Dale Jr., is one of the most popular drivers in NASCAR today. Junior has a driving style a lot like his father's. Through Junior, the Earnhardt name and tradition of winning continues.

Career Highlights

1970   Dale drives in his first pro race.

1974   Dale drives his first race on a paved track in the Sportsman division.

1975   Dale races for the first time in a Cup race in Charlotte, North Carolina.

1979   Dale races his first full year in NASCAR's top series. He wins two races and the Rookie of the Year award.

1980   Dale wins more than a half million dollars and his first Cup Series championship.

1986   Dale wins five races and the Cup Series championship.

1987   Dale wins 11 races, plus the All-Star race and the Cup Series championship.

1994   Dale wins his fourth Cup Series championship in five years, his seventh overall.

1998   Dale wins the Daytona 500 for the first time.

2001   Dale is killed in a crash on the last lap of the Daytona 500.

Glossary

aggressive (uh-GRESS-iv)—strong and forceful

dominate (DOM-uh-nate)—to control or rule

pavement (PAYV-muhnt)—a hard material, such as concrete or asphalt, that is used to cover roads or sidewalks

sedan (si-DAN)—a style of closed car that has a hard top and doors

welder (WELD-ur)—a person whose job it is to join pieces of metal together with heat

Read More

Barber, Phil. *Dale Earnhardt: The Likable Intimidator.* The World of NASCAR. Excelsior, Minn.: Tradition Books, 2003.

McHugh, A. R. *Dale Earnhardt.* Sports Superstars. Chanhassen, Minn.: Child's World, 2001.

Moore, Bob. *Dale Earnhardt.* NASCAR Wonderboy Collector Series. Chicago: Triumph Books, 2002.

Internet Sites

FactHound offers a safe, fun way to find Internet sites related to this book. All of the sites on FactHound have been researched by our staff.

Here's how:

1. Visit *www.facthound.com*

2. Choose your grade level.

3. Type in this book ID **0736843779** for age-appropriate sites. You may also browse subjects by clicking on letters, or by clicking on pictures and words.

4. Click on the **Fetch It** button.

FactHound will fetch the best sites for you!

Index